CHRISTIAN DUTIES

ZENAS TRIVETT

INTRODUCTION BY MICHAEL HAYKIN

CHRISTIAN DUTIES

ZENAS TRIVETT

INTRODUCTION BY MICHAEL HAYKIN

1791

FREE GRACE PRESS

Christian Duties

Zenas Trivett

Original title: Plain Christian Duties recommended, in an exhortation delivered at the settlement of a church of the Baptist denomination,
on 22d of March 1790, and now published, by
request, for the benefit of Christians in general,
and members of churches in particular.

Originally published in Sudbury, 1791
by W. Brackett.

Reprinted and updated by
Free Grace Press, 2021
1076 Harkrider Street
Conway AR 72032

Cover design by Rick Smith

Printed in the UK by 4edge Limited
ISBN: 978-1-952599-33-0

Contents

Plain Christian Duties Recommended, in an exhortation delivered at the settlement of a church of the Baptist denomination, on 22nd of March 1790, and now published, by request, for the benefit of Christians in general, and members of churches in particular.

Introduction

The Life and Ministry
of Zenas Trivett—a Sketch by
Michael Haykin

In the anonymous obituary written for Zenas
Trivett (1753–1831) in *The Baptist Magazine*, its
author indicated his desire for any of his readers
who could write "a more prolonged memoir"
than he had done to do so. Sadly, none was forth-
coming. The materials we have, then, for even
a small biographical sketch like this are spare at
best.[1]

---

1   See the bibliography for available material.

Trivett grew up in the robust Baptist work in Worstead, Norfolk, where his father Edward Trivett (1712–1792) was the pastor of the church for many years. Converted in 1775 and baptized in May of that year, Zenas began to preach the following year. One of his early converts was a woman named Esther Rogers, who was saved in 1776 through a sermon that he preached on Revelation 6:17 ("The great day of his wrath is come") at Eythorne, Kent. Two years later, in 1778, he assumed the pastorate of the Baptist church in Langham, Essex, which he pastored for forty years until his retirement in 1819. Ten years after Trivett retired from Langham, the congregation numbered around 450, the bulk of whom had been added during Trivett's ministry.

With his good friend Thomas Steevens (1745–1802) of Colchester, Trivett was involved in the formation of the Essex Baptist Association in 1796, which provided a vehicle for church planting and revitalization in the county. Prior to this, his church had been involved in the Norfolk and Suffolk Association. Trivett continued to attend the annual meetings of the Norfolk and

Suffolk Association after the formation of the Essex Baptist Association. Trivett was also a strong supporter of the Bristol Baptist Academy and the Baptist Missionary Society and was a signatory at the meeting that set up the first Baptist Union in 1812. His involvement in these various endeavors brought him into the circle of Baptist leaders associated with Andrew Fuller (1754–1815), John Ryland Jr. (1753–1825), and Thomas Steevens. Fuller met Trivett on a number of occasions and treasured his friendship.

Trivett appears to have published only two works: a broadsheet entitled *A Scheme of Chronology representing at one View, the Times of the Prophets, and how long they Prophesied* (1794) and this work, *Plain Christian Duties Recommended* (1791), which is an address that Trivett gave at the establishment of a new congregation and which was issued in a second edition in 1794 by the London Baptist publisher William Button (1754–1821). This small pamphlet lays out the various responsibilities of a faithful member of a local church. Not surprisingly, Trivett emphasized that congregational polity was "the alone [i.e., only] plan of the New Testament," though he urged his hearers never to dream that "all true religion [is] confined to your own denomination." Trivett's call to the congregation to often "meet together … for prayer and conversation" is particularly germane in our day of online digital streaming. For often believers who had come together "destitute of the spirit of devotion," Trivett noted, have "had their cold affections warmed."

Extracts of the Langham Church's letter written by Trivett to the annual meeting of the Essex Baptist Association in 1801 are also preserved in John Rippon's (1751–1836) *The Baptist Annual Register* for 1801 and 1802. In it, Trivett rejoiced in the establishment of a new work at the small market town of Thorpe (now Thorpe-le-Soken), about fourteen miles away toward Harwich. Over the course of a week in November of the following year (November 10–17, 1802) Trivett played a large public role in the ordination of this church's first pastor, W. Bolton, and the opening of their church building for worship. The church was formally opened for worship on November 10, and that Lord's Day, November 14, Trivett preached what was described as "an impressive discourse" from Philippians 1:27. Bolton was ordained the following Wednesday, November 17, and Trivett preached what were the customary two sermons—one to the ordinand and one to the congregation—as one address without a set text, which was somewhat unusual. The record of the ordination service was thus described: "It was a good day."

1

Recommended

As you have requested me to address you on the present occasion, I hope you will suffer the word of exhortation. You are this day become a Church of Jesus Christ. Formed not by coercion and compulsion, but on the noble principles of Christian liberty; "stand firm therefore in the liberty by which Christ has made you free" (Gal. 5:1).

Your conduct today reproves and confutes the common vulgar ideal that a church is a building composed of wood and stone, in which men meet to worship God. Your practice declares that not the building, but the true worshipers therein, properly united, are the church. Your conduct today also opposes the idea of a national church, and you agree with the Church of England that a church of Christ is a congregation of faithful men, not a nation of faithless infidels.

You also renounce the idea of a parochial church, having chosen the congregational form, and embodied on that plan which is the alone plan of the New Testament. Indeed, the inhabitants of a parish, as well as those of a nation, are not fit to form a church of Christ, which is a habitation for the Most High, and will appear very evidently by an inspection of their character and conduct. Where is the parish that will admit of an exception?

Be thankful, my brothers, that you are taught a plan of church order and government that does not lead you to hold fellowship and communion with drunkards, fornicators, liars, extortioners, unjust, and profane persons, but you admit whom you please to your communion, and have power to reject those whom you judge unworthy.

You, this day, are a church of Jesus Christ, a dwelling place for the God of Jacob, for God has said of Zion, "This is my resting place forever; Here I will dwell, for I have desired it" (Ps. 132:14).

God's church is His house, but it is a spiritual house, built with living and lively stones, which are united together with the cement of love. Ezekiel seems to have had a vision of the gospel-church under the idea of a house, when God commanded him to "describe the temple to the house of Israel, that they may be ashamed of their iniquities; and let them measure the pattern. And if they are ashamed of all that they have done, make known to them the design of the temple and its arrangement, its exits and its entrances, its entire design and all its ordinances, all its forms and all its laws" (Ezek. 43:10–12).

Now, as you have become a house of God, there is reason to hope and expect that some who love and long for the divine presence will seek admission among you; to admit new members into a gospel-church is pleasing work, but it requires much caution, for while some come with sincere hearts, and pure intentions, with a desire to feed among the sheep, and to enjoy and glorify the great Shepherd, others probably will be prompted by base motives and sinister ends, seeking not God's glory but their own honor or interest. Be not, therefore, too hasty, my friends, in the admission of members into your society. The way of entrance into the house of God is by faith in Christ, who is the door of that house. Be well satisfied that the persons you admit are believers in Christ, and such who prove their faith by their works.

On the other hand, be very careful that you grieve not such as are weak in faith and understanding, by rejecting them on that account. Remember, if you have evidence that they are gracious souls, that is sufficient, for the great King of Zion never intended that His children should become men before they are admitted into His visible kingdom. The church of Christ is a sheepfold and is intended for the protection and benefit of His lambs, as well as His sheep. It is a nursery into which babes are to be received and where they are to be fed with the sincere milk of the word, that they may grow from babes to men, and so to fathers in the church of God.

To see a company of such babes flocking to the house of God, and to hear them there lisp out His goodness, tell of His grace, and say, "Come, and let us join ourselves to the Lord in a perpetual covenant that shall not be forgotten"—O how delightful!

But I must leave this pleasing scene and turn your attention to another. Though it is a painful scene, it is nevertheless necessary to be attended to; permit me, then, to observe that notwithstanding all your vigilance and care, probably some conniving hypocrite will find a way into your community, whose hypocrisy may afterwards be detected. Or perhaps someone who shall have been of considerable standing there may walk contrary to his profession and dishonor God: in both these cases it will be necessary to admonish and reprove. If admonition fails to answer the desired end, and is disregarded, it will then be necessary to proceed to severer measures, and to remember that there is a way out of the church as well as into it: "Son of man," says the Lord, "shew them the goings out thereof" (Ezek. 43:10–11).

An unworthy and dishonorable member of a church of Christ is like a distempered limb, which being mortified, endangers the whole body to which it is united, and therefore must be cut off, lest the whole body should be infected and perish.

This work, as we have said, however painful, must be attended to in certain cases, otherwise, we shall be partakers of other men's sins, retain that reproach which in measure might be wiped away, and offend God, by conniving at iniquity. But then, like skillful surgeons, we should never use the knife until all other means fail.

Permit me here to add, if you should ever have to exercise this trying part of church discipline, take care that your motives are right. Let them be not self-willed and revengeful but aimed at the glory of God, the purification of the church, and the good of the offender. For it would be very unbecoming and imprudent in us to exercise our evil passions in a part of discipline which we ourselves may have to undergo, and if not kept by an almighty power most certainly shall deserve.

You have this day separated yourselves from the world, and by professing to be a church of Jesus Christ declared that you are not of the world. From this day, the eyes of the world will be upon you, the wicked will watch for your halting. They will observe your steps closely. If they find anything in your conduct that is criminal, they will not fail to report it, and to represent it, too, in a light not the most favorable to your interest. They will triumph in your miscarriages, crying, "Ah, so would we have it. These are your professors? We don't see that they are better than any others. Ah, they're all alike."

How careful then, my dear friends, should you be that you give them no just cause for censure and reproach. No reason to speak evil of the professors of religion on your account, no room to judge unfavorably of the cause you profess, by the irregularity of your conduct. It seems the very thought of bringing a reproach upon the cause you are this day embarked in is almost ready to break your hearts. You say, "Lord, let me rather die than sin against you, and dishonor your cause, and wound the hearts of your dear children." May the Lord grant that softness of heart, and may tenderness of conscience remain to excite in you watchfulness throughout all your pilgrimage.

Endeavor so to conduct yourselves in all your dealings in connections that the men of the world may not have to say that your religion will not make you honest tradesmen, nor good neighbors.

That in spite of all your pretensions to satisfy, you can overreach in your bargains, falsify your promises, and quarrel with your neighbors.

But as you profess to be the disciples of Christ, let it be seen that your conduct is regulated by your Master's rule, who has said "Therefore, whatever you want men to do to you, do also to them, for this is the Law and the Prophets" (Matt. 7:12). An admirable rule calculated to solve a thousand difficulties! What way of judging, so accurate, what method of determining, so safe, as putting ourselves in the place of others, while we consider them in ours, before we pass sentence? To say all that respects your conduct toward the men of the world in one word, "Let your light so shine before men, that they may see your good works and glorify your Father in heaven" (Matt. 5:16).

In the next place, my friends, permit me to add a word or two respecting your conduct toward the professors of religion of other denominations. Be careful then that you give no one room to suspect that you consider all true religion confined to your own denomination. If you profess to see further than some others, and know more than they, do not despise them, nor pride yourselves in your own wisdom, but be humble and thankful. What have you that you have not received? Were you not once as ignorant as others? If there is any difference, who has made you to differ? Is it not by the grace of God that you are what you are? "Now if you did indeed receive it, why do you boast as if you had not received it?" (1 Cor. 4:7).

There was a time when you did not see many things which you now see, so there may be a time when others shall increase in knowledge as much as you have done. And remember, he is not always the greatest Christian that knows the most, but he that obeys the best.

Love all of every denomination in whom you can discern the lovely image of your blessed Lord. That so doing, you may obtain that honorable character, "a lover of what is good" (Titus 1:8). Is it not unreasonable, as well as uncharitable, that men who agree in ten points should live in the neglect of Christian love because they disagree in one?

Let me add by way of caution, let every man's conscience bear him this testimony, that he is not aiming to promote his own cause, more than the cause of Jesus Christ. Brothers, you undoubtedly think you are right, this brings you satisfaction, but remember, it affords no proof to others that you are so. Let the excellency of your religion be evidenced by the kindness of your dispositions, and the uniformity of your lives. Unite with all good men endeavoring to promote the common cause of our Lord and Savior, Jesus Christ.

You are this day becoming a church of Jesus Christ. Having, I hope, first given your own selves unto the Lord, you have now, in the presence of the great God, and this congregation, given yourselves one to another.

Suffer me then to observe that new relations and connections create new duties and obligations. It is the same in natural relations. There are duties incumbent on the child, but when this child arrives at manhood, and has become a husband, other duties devolve upon him. Immediately as he becomes a father, duties of another kind claim his attention. So it is in civil connections. One kind of duties are incumbent on the servant, if he commences to become a master, another sort, and if he arrives at office and becomes a magistrate, a third class requires his observance. So also it is in connections in relations of a spiritual kind. You are this day entered into a near relation to each other, you are becoming brothers and sisters in one church.

Give me leave, then, to observe that many and great as your duties might appear before, they are this day greatly increased. My business now will be to point out these duties, and inculcate an observance of them. May the Lord help me to speak, and you to hear.

2

Love

The first of these duties which I would inculcate is love. This is the very essence of true religion, and the necessary prerequisite to a Christian conduct. Without this it is impossible to do our duty, either toward God, or toward one another. If you become destitute of love, your profession is vain, and you are neither likely to glorify God nor edify each other.

This may be called a foundational duty, it being that on which the right performance of every other duty depends. The more we love, the more we are like God, for "God is love" (1 John 4:8). What can we aim at so honorable and so excellent as to bear a likeness to the Deity? Here, then, as in all other cases, duty and privilege are united.

To this duty, my dear friends, I hope you will not fail to pay a particular attention. For how sad must be the case for those professors, who, while they commune together, and commemorate the love of Christ, are destitute of love themselves! I ask, is there likely to be a blessing on their union in communion? I fear not. Let your conduct to each other be such, that while others behold it, they may say, "See how these Christians love one another!"

Consider, my friends, how great are your obligations to the performance of this duty; Christ your dear Savior has commanded it, saying, "A new commandment I give to you, that you love one another; as I have loved you, that you also love one another" (John 13:34). Do you hope that you are the objects of Christ's love? Let this love then constrain you to love one another. Again, remember, Christ has set the example, for he who has commanded you to love the saints, has loved them himself infinitely more than you do.

Can you look upon a brother or sister, and believe that Christ has so loved them as to die for them, and feel no love for them yourselves? I hope it is otherwise with you. Again, consider, you are brothers, children of the same father, heirs of the same inheritance, purchased with the same blood, are traveling the same road, hoping for the same salvation, and expecting to dwell together forever.

Let me add, that you are also members one of another. As the Apostle has said, you are the body of Christ, and members in particular. This near relation then, ought to be considered as a stimulus to love. Does the Apostle say, "He who loves his wife loves himself" (Eph. 5:28)? So he that loves the church, loves that body of which he himself is a member.

In attending to this duty, you will bring glory to God, and be happy yourselves, and make others happy also. For, "behold, how good and how pleasant it is for brothers to dwell together in unity!" (Ps. 133:1). If this love is due to all the saints, it cannot be less so to those of your own community, but as the relation is in some respects nearer, so the affection ought to be in some respects stronger.

3

Sympathy

If we love our fellow members, we will be ready to sympathize with them and all their troubles. The pilgrim's path is often a rough and thorny way. For it is, "through many tribulations enter the kingdom of God" (Acts 14:22), and "many are the afflictions of the righteous" (Ps. 34:19). These afflictions are frequently both of body and mind.

Now in all these troubles and afflictions you ought to sympathize with them. Perhaps a very considerable assistance may not be in your power to give them, but hard is that heart that cannot pay one short visit, that cannot afford one look of pity, to a poor afflicted brother.

There he lies, on a bed of languishing, scorched with a burning fever, wracked with acute pains, or wasted with a pining sickness. The cries of his all but fatherless children pierce his ears, but more his heart, while he feels his enfeebled hand unable to supply their wants. And the partner of his cares has her heart torn in two by the strength of conjugal affection and the power of maternal love.

Here is another of your brothers, whose pitiful case asks all the tender feelings of your sympathetic hearts. He has grieved the Holy Spirit, and has lost the presence of his God. With the departure of the son of righteousness, in his all-gladdening rays, did all his joys depart. His evidences are clouded. His hopes of heaven are fled. He almost concludes that he shall no more see one cheerful day. Little more remains, in his apprehension, "but a certain fearful expectation of judgment, and fiery indignation which will devour the adversaries" (Heb. 10:27).

Ah! My brothers, can you pass these solitary cells, these melancholy cottages, without turning in to bear, by sympathy, a part of the burdens of their disconsolate inhabitants and drop some cheering word, to support their sinking minds, and heal their broken hearts? How excellent was the disposition of the great Apostle, who could say, "Who is weak, and I am not weak? Who is made to stumble, and I do not burn with indignation?" (2 Cor. 11:29). Admirable spirit! Blessed disciple of the compassionate Savior, who left us this excellent example! Imitate the apostle, brothers: "Bear one another's burdens, and so fulfill the law of Christ" (Gal. 6:2).

4

Generosity

Our love and sympathy can never be made to appear genuine without generosity, at least, if we have it in our own power to share. What proof of love does that man give, who only says to his poor destitute brother, "Depart in peace, be warmed and filled," but does not open his hand to participate in his brother's necessity.

How deplorable had been our case, brothers, if Christ had only pitied us, and not added participation to His compassion! We would have been forever miserable. Follow the example of Christ then, brothers, and to your sympathy add generosity.

The primitive Christians had weekly collections for the poor, they had compassion on the fatherless, and provided for the widow, 'the blessing of a perishing man came upon me" (Job 29:13). Shall we steel our hearts, and stand all the day idle? Open your ears, my brothers, and with them your hearts, to the crying necessity of pinching poverty, and do not turn your eyes from beholding the ones of the destitute.

There is a poor brother whose hungry stomach, when fed by the hand of your generosity, would rejoice to bless you. Can your heart be so hard, unfeeling, and stupid, as to deny relief to his necessities, and prevent his grateful heart from blessing you?

There is a poor sister whose heart heaves with sorrow for the loss of an affectionate and indulgent husband. By his industrious hand she has been accustomed to have her own, and her family's, necessities supplied. But now, one grave has swallowed up the husband and the father, and together with him, all her hopes of earthly comfort. His lips, now cold and silent, no more drop the wholesome words of instruction to the mother and her children, nor his hands provide their necessary food. The fatherless children are left to feel the miseries of pinching necessity while their sad sorrows increase the swelling anguish of their widowed mother's heart, which is overborn with grief.

Can you imagine that these sad scenes require your sympathy alone? Do they not also demand your assistance? Is not God hereby giving you opportunity to prove the sincerity of your love? To give evidence before God and men that your hearts are not destitute of Christian charity? Remember the words of the beloved Disciple: "Whoever has this world's goods, and sees his brother in need, and shuts up his heart from him, how does the love of God abide in him?" (1 John 3:17). Let me add, with that affectionate Apostle, "My little children, let us not love in word or in tongue, but in deed and in truth" (1 John 3:18).

Well then, brothers, "do not forget to do good and to share" and for your encouragement remember, "with such sacrifices God is well pleased" (Heb. 13:16).

When your Lord comes the second time, and calls the whole world to judgment, and says to you, "Come, you blessed of My Father, inherit the kingdom prepared for you from the foundation of the world: for I was hungry and you gave Me food; I was thirsty and you gave Me drink; I was a stranger and you took Me in; I was naked and you clothed Me; I was sick and you visited Me" (Matt. 25:34–36).

When you find, by happy experience, that what you do for Christ's poor children, he takes it as done unto himself, and that the small gift of "a cup of cold water, shall by no means lose" (Matt. 10:42) its reward, you will not then think you have done too much for the poor of Christ's flock.

5

Impartiality

See that you be not partial, brothers, for if you are respecters of persons, all your generosity will not give satisfaction. For, if while one is remembered but another be forgotten, this will cause grief and uneasiness, and perhaps disgust. Take care that you give no fellow member occasion to say, "Ah! They have no respect for me. I'm looked upon as an outcast here, and I fear I will be one soon." Avoid him crying to God, and there be found sin in you.

Be careful, if you are called to judge in any matter, between two fellow members, not to pervert justice through partiality. It does not matter what difference there may be between the parties as to worldly circumstances.

Be careful also that you do not divide into parties, through partiality. For divisions will create prejudices and then farewell peace and happiness. If you give the preference to any, besides such as are in office, let it be to the aged. "The silver-haired head is a crown of glory, if it is found in the way of righteousness" (Prov. 16:31). Also, to the man that bears most his Savior's image, for he is most worthy to be honored.

Take heed also that you not be partial to yourselves. So while you behold the speck that is in your brother's eye that you do not see the plank that is in your own eye.

Be impartial also in your attention to the divine commands, and while you attend to one, see to it that you do not neglect another. "Do nothing with partiality" (1 Tim. 5:21), brothers, for, "the wisdom that is from above is without partiality" (James 3:17).

Therefore, "do not hold the faith of our Lord Jesus Christ, the Lord of glory, with partiality"

(James 2:1). On the other hand, be very careful that none of you suspect partiality, where it is not used, nor intended.

6

Peace

This is a duty of great consequence in the church of God. For no longer than peace is maintained, may you expect prosperity. Once a church of Christ, which ought to be a quiet and peaceable habitation, becomes a house of strife and contention, the members look upon one another as enemies instead of friends, and strangers instead of brothers. What can then be expected, but "confusion, and every evil thing?" (James 3:16). Is it reasonable then to expect prosperity?

Doesn't the blessed Spirit reject the seats of wrath and clamor? Woe to that church from

which he departs! Will young converts, whose
hearts are full of love to the sons of peace, be as
ready to join the children of strife? Will the real
lovers of peace be willing to unite and fellowship
with the promoters of contention? Or will they not
rather dread the thought of being connected with
such a people? If then, you wish for happiness and
prosperity, brothers, "endeavor to keep the unity
of the Spirit in the bond of peace" (Eph. 4:3).

Consider also, you professed to be the subjects
of the Prince of peace and the children of the
God of peace. How unbecoming your character,
and how contrary to your profession do you act,
when, instead of manifesting a peaceable disposition you evidence the contrary. Remember the
advice of Joseph to his brothers, "see that you do
not become troubled along the way."

Let not little things be the occasion of disputes
in contentions among you. Remember, the peace
of the church is too valuable to be disturbed in
order to gratify the mood and whim of any indi-
vidual. Every church member ought to prefer the
peace of the church to the gratification of his own
temper.

I am aware that the angry man, who is heated by passion, and blinded by prejudice, will reply, "but it is truth that I'm contending for." I ask, what pure truth, without any mixture of self-will? Look narrowly, examine closely, it is more than possible that some evil passion may hide itself under the specious name of zeal for God. If truth is your object, so it is your brother's too.

You would wish your brother to conform his faith to your standard, but he possesses an equal right to require the same of you, which is in fact no right at all. You wish the liberty of judging for yourself. Give him that liberty, he asked no more, that you are bound to give by the great author of Christian liberty. For he has said, "whatever you want men to do to you, do also to them, for this is the Law and the Prophets" (Matt. 7:12).

Can it be reasonable to yield to unreasonable requirements? Ask no more of your brother than is reasonable, no more than you are willing that he should require of you. Then you will probably not be denied.

Remember, brothers, "how great a forest a little fire kindles" (James 3:5) and "The beginning

of strife is like releasing water; therefore stop contention before a quarrel starts" (Prov. 17:14). It is
very easy to break peace, but very hard to restore
it. Therefore, "If it is possible as depends on
you, live peaceably with all men" (Rom. 12:18).
Endeavor to cultivate the same among yourselves,
"and the God of love and peace will be with you"
(2 Cor. 13:11).

7

Self-Denial

He who will not use self-denial can never make a peaceable member of society. For men in a state of imperfect knowledge can never all see alike, and it would be unreasonable to expect it. Proud nature, far from compliant, does not like to yield. Without the exercise of self-denial there must be an end of peace. For where men see differently, in many cases they will act differently.

If it be in a matter of church discipline, there will most likely be a majority on one side, and consequently a minority on the other, whose duty, no doubt, it is to submit to the greater number. Submission calls for self-denial, and which in such a case ought to be exercised, and rendered without murmuring.

Self-denial is essential to Christianity, it is the Christian's duty, when he is considered personally. When he becomes a member of a Christian society, duty binds him to exercise it differently.

There may be some part of the conduct of some of you, which in your apprehension, and in itself, may be innocent, but it may not be so in the view of some of your brothers, their minds, being weak, may be hurt by it. Now in such a case we ought to use self-denial, or else we "no longer walk in love" (Rom. 14:15). As Paul says, "We then who are strong ought to bear with the scruples of the weak, and not to please ourselves" (Rom. 15:1).

According to this rule the Apostle himself determinded to act, for, although "I knew and was convinced by the Lord Jesus, that there was nothing unclean of itself" (Rom. 14:14), yet, so great was his charity and self-denial, that "if food makes my brother stumble, I will never again eat meat, lest I make my brother stumble" (1 Cor. 8:13).

Excellent example! Let us copy it, my brothers. Let us "look out not only for his own interest, but also for the interest of others" (Phil. 2:4). Let us not be self-willed, but "submitting to one another in the fear of God" (Eph. 5:21).

8

Humility

On humility depends the exercise of self-denial, for the proud man thinks it too great a stoop for him, to deny himself for the sake of others. While the man who is little in his own eyes can easily submit to others and deny himself for their advantage. He does not think himself of so much consequence that everything must give way to him. He is unassuming, in many cases, of his own judgment, and therefore can more easily bear contradiction than the proud and confident.

Humility is an excellent grace, it makes the disciple like his Lord and master, who was "gentle and lowly" (Matt. 11:29), and whose lovely image it is our greatest honor to resemble. Is it possible that we should be his disciples without humility? Would it not imply a contradiction to say such a one is a proud disciple of the humble Savior? Pride is abhorrent to God, and disgraceful to men, but humility is the Christian's ornament.

The Apostle Peter therefore says, "you younger people, submit yourselves to your elders. Yes, all of you be submissive to one another, and be clothed with humility, for God resists the proud, but gives grace to the humble" (1 Peter 5:5).

How disgraceful is it for a man who bears the honorable character of a member of a church of Christ (and who therefore is expected to exercise all humility) to swell with pride, show a condescending presence, grow up into a Diotrephes, and lord it over God's heritage, wanting in everything to bear the control. Who seeks to convert a society of free Christians into a company of slaves, over which he himself becomes a petty tyrant. Shouldn't such a man tremble at the proverb, "Pride goes before destruction, and a haughty spirit before a fall" (Prov. 16:18)?

Do not assume the appearance of masters in the church of God, but like him who washed the disciples' feet, let each one take "upon him the form of a servant" (Phil. 2:7), and "let nothing be done through selfish ambition, or conceit, but in lowliness of mind let each esteem others better than himself" (Phil. 2:3).

9

Prayer

The next duty which I would instill is prayer. Prayer is, by some divines, called the breath of the Christian. Indeed, the Christian lives no longer than he prays. When once he begins to neglect this duty, he begins to die, and no longer lives as a Christian.

Prayer is the duty of every Christian, but members of churches have particular connections, and are therefore under peculiar obligations to this duty. It is not only their duty to remember Zion in general, but to pray for the church to which they belong in particular. They ought to pray that the word preached among them may be blessed to their brothers, as well as to themselves, that their brothers may grow in grace, as well as themselves. Also, that God would bless the word for the conversion of sinners. Increase the church, by adding to it daily, such as shall be saved.

It is also their duty to pay special attention to particular cases. The churches of Christ are seldom long without their trials. These trials should be brought by every member of the church to the throne of grace. It is there where direction, assistance, and deliverance should be sought.

Moreover, inquiry should be made into the particular cases of your fellow members. Each one should bear upon your hearts before God. If you find any of your brothers or sisters under affliction, or any heavy trials or temptations, let such by no means be forgotten in your prayers. For your encouragement, remember he that has said, "The effective fervent prayer of a righteous man avails much" (James 5:16).

Can you see a poor fellow member laboring under the weight of a heavy affliction? Or hear him groaning under the power of some sore temptation, and not lend him the kind assistance of your prayers? Pray hard for one another. Also, pray with one another, and no doubt you shall be answered. Christ has said, "if two of you agree on earth concerning anything that they ask, it will be done for them by my Father in heaven" (Matt. 18:19). Believe the promise, distrust His word no more.

10

Watchfulness

It is not sufficient that you pray, but you must also watch. Both of these united will not be found more than sufficient to guard you against the snares of the world, the assaults of the devil, and the lust of the flesh. These are powerful enemies, and to withstand them will require all your vigilance.

Remember, others are watching you. The wicked are watching for you to falter. This should make you the more watchful of yourselves. Also, "your adversary the devil walks about like a roaring lion, seeking whom he may devour" (1 Peter 5:8). The eyes of other Christians are also upon you. Above all remember, the eye of a holy God is always upon you, beholding all your conduct.

Let these considerations excite you to watchfulness. And be careful to watch the first motions of sin in your hearts, that you may quench the spark of sin before it be kindled into a flame. "Watch and pray, lest you enter into temptation" (Matt. 26:41).

Let me add, it is your duty also to watch over one another. Not with a view to pick up something in order to reproach each other, but let it be in love. With a view to prevent any disgrace that might be brought upon the cause of Christ, through the misconduct of a fellow member. I'll conclude this article with the words of Christ, "What I say to you, I say to all: Watch!" (Mark 13:37).

11

Forbearance

In exercising the duty of watchfulness over one another, you may probably discern something amiss in the conduct of a Christian brother. However, it may not be a capital offense. In such a case, you are not to be rash and hasty, but to use forbearance. You are not to make a man an offender for a word, but call to mind your own infirmities, and remember how much you need forbearance, both from God and man.

Is your brother in an error? Perhaps he does not see it. If he did, he would probably desire to forsake it as much as you are that he should. You should not severely rebuke him, instead, instruct him with meekness. For you yourself have often times been in error, your own heart can testify without a doubt.

Brothers, call to remembrance the words of the Apostle, "Therefore, as the elect of God, holy and beloved, put on tender mercies, kindness, humility, meekness, longsuffering; bearing with one another, and forgiving one another" (Col. 3:12–13). Cover, with the mantle of love, the common infirmities of your brothers. But if their offense be more capital, then I must recommend to you another duty, admonition.

12

Admonition

There are some offenses of too heinous a nature to be overlooked, and passed by in silence. Indeed, it would be wrong they should, for that would be to suffer sin upon our brother, which the Word of God forbids. Your duty, in these cases, will be to admonish and reprove. However, be careful to proceed according to the Scripture rule, for admonition is a very difficult duty, and to give reproof properly requires great wisdom and caution. Endeavor then to study the Word of God respecting this matter.

Allow me to recommend to your attentions the following rule, laid down by our Lord. "If your brother sins against you, go and tell him his fault between you and him alone. If he hears you, you have gained your brother. But if he will not hear, take with you one or two more, that 'by the mouth of two or three witnesses every word may be established.' And if he refuses to hear them, tell it to the church. But if he refuses even to hear the church, let him be to you like a heathen and a tax collector" (Matt. 18:15–17).

Observe, you are not to make public your brother's offense, unless necessity require it, but to endeavor to show him what he has done wrong. If he confesses his fault, forgive him, and let the injury die. Let no one know it, without necessity. Be particularly careful not to make anything church business until you be obliged to do it. There has been a world of mischief made by bringing every trifling thing before the church. The rule we have just adverted to gives no acceptability to such a practice, but quite the contrary.

The spirit in which admonitions are to be given and received also requires your attention. For on this, success very much depends. If angry passions are predominant in your admonitions, they will most likely render all you say of no effect. For you will generally find that the same spirit which you manifest will be begotten in your friend. Admonitions given in an angry spirit will be received in anger, and such as are given in love will be much the more likely to be received in love.

Besides, how very unbecoming and imprudent is it, for a man that is subject to infirmities and liable to admonitions himself, to go to a fallen brother in the spirit of anger, as though he himself had never been guilty of a single crime, nor ever should. How contrary is this to the apostolic rule, "Brethren, if a man is overtaken in any trespass, you who are spiritual restore such a one in a spirit of gentleness, considering yourself lest you also be tempted" (Gal. 6:1). Is your brother fallen? "You stand by faith. Do not be haughty, but fear" (Rom. 11:20).

Again, admonitions ought to be received in love. They are intended for the benefit of the person who receives them, and should be considered as acts of friendship and brotherly kindness. If a brother converts me from the error of my way, instrumentally, he saves my "soul from death and cover a multitude of sins" (James 5:20). Let us say with David, "Let the righteous strike me; it shall be a kindness. And let him rebuke me; it shall be as excellent oil; let my head not refuse it. For still my prayer is against the deeds of the wicked" (Ps. 141:5).

To say all in a word, let all your admonitions be given in love, and be sure to let your brother see that your design is not to reproach him but to restore him. While one brother becomes a wise and affectionate reprover, let the other lend an obedient ear.

13

Forgiveness

It is inevitable that offenses will come. Therefore when they do come, we should be prepared to receive them. They should not be received by indulging and cherishing a spirit of resentment, but by steady determination not to be "overcome by evil, but overcome evil with good" (Rom. 12:21).

Let us not be surprised at offenses. For what reason can we have to expect that everybody should entertain our inclination, and give way to us? Are we persons of so much consequence? It is then probably in our own eyes, and not in the eyes of others. If any of you wish to appear great, then let him exercise forgiveness. He will not only appear great, but be so. For "it is a man's glory to overlook a transgression" (Prov. 19:11) and "he who rules his spirit is better than he who takes a city" (Prov. 16:32).

Consider, my friends, how reasonable is this duty. But what folly and madness is displayed in a contrary conduct. Here is a brother who has offended you, probably without intention. However, your overheated spirit imputes it to design. He is willing to make concessions, and seeks a reconciliation, but you cannot be reconciled. You cannot forgive. Your prejudiced mind considers his repentance as feigned and his humiliation as hypocritical. And, until your stony, unrelenting heart be softened, in vain does he show the true tokens of sincerity.

Let me ask you, inconsiderate mortal! How do you approach a throne of grace? How do you draw near to God, the Searcher of all hearts? Can you hide from Him the hardness of your heart? Can you ask forgiveness, and yet not forgive? Should your heart presume to ask the important blessing, can you think it will be granted? Or have you forgotten the positive declaration of the lips of truth?

Remember, he has said, "if you do not forgive men their trespasses, neither will your Father forgive your trespasses" (Matt. 6:15). One would think that he who reads these words seriously would not dare to close his eyes and sleep, until he had from his heart, freely and fully, forgiven all who had offended him. Lest awakening no more in this world, he should appear before God unforgiven, with all his sins about him.

How excellent then is the advice of Paul, "do not let the sun go down on your wrath, nor give place to the devil" (Eph. 4:26–27). I remember having heard of two good men who on some occasion had a quarrel. Remembering this exhortation of the Apostle, just before sunset, one of them went to the other, and knocking at the door, his offended friend came and opened it, in seeing who it was, started back with resentment and surprise, the other at the same time cried out, "The sun is almost down." This unexpected situation softened the heart of his friend into affection, and he returned for answer, "Come in brother, come in." What an example, brothers! Let us do ourselves the honor to follow it.

Is it generally allowed, I presume, that our Lord's prayer was intended as a directory for us? If so, then we ought always to cultivate a spirit agreeable to that, and never cherish a disposition that would prevent our using it. How is the man that cannot forgive his brother to use this petition, "Forgive us our debts, as we forgive our debtors" (Matt. 6:12)? Such a man forgives not at all, and therefore to pray to be forgiven as he forgives is to pray that he may not be forgiven at all. If he be not forgiven, his sins will sink him down to everlasting torments.

Think, then, of the advice of Christ, and forgive, before you ask forgiveness. But I think some of you are saying, "We have forgiven, once, and again. Still offenses are repeated. How often would you have us forgive?" Peter said, "up to seven times" but Peter's Lord, "up to seventy times seven" (Matt. 18:21–22). My brothers, what will become of us, if God forgives us but seven offenses! Surely hell must be our portion. Well, then, "if anyone has a complaint against another; even as Christ forgave you, so you also must do" (Col. 3:13), that is, freely, fully, and forever, never to abrade you with it more. This leads me to another duty which is union.

14

Union

Christians, especially members of the same church, ought to unite together. Brothers, let it not be said that your "contentions are like the bars of a castle" (Prov. 18:19), that you cannot yield. Let it be seen, that you are like "willows by the water-courses" (Isa. 44:4), whose pliant branches gently bow, and mutually yield to embrace each other.

Unite together, and meet as opportunity shall offer. Not only for public worship, but also for social duties. For remember, the various services which you owe each other can never be performed unless you meet and unite together. If you keep at a distance, how are you to unite in prayer, edify, and watch over one another? Social meetings are very profitable. Where they are neglected, we generally find a want of zeal for God. Such churches seldom flourish, but on the contrary we generally see the members of such a society grow cold and lifeless.

Christians, like burning coals, soon lose their warmth and fervor when parted from each other. Bring them near together, and each conspires to give and receive a mutual glow, so that the whole is all on fervent flame.

Meet together, my friends, for prayer and conversation. How often has it been seen that a company of Christians, who met together dull and stupid, carnal and lukewarm, destitute of the spirit of devotion, and having neither heart nor tongue for God, have had their cold affections warmed, their hard hearts made soft, their languid hopes revived, their beclouded evidences brightened, and their mouths filled with heavenly praise and have parted full of joy.

While one relates the pleasing story of his conversion with melting heart and flowing eyes, another is eager to receive the whole and thrust forward his head big with expectation, while he feels his sympathetic soul kindle into love. A third communicates his spiritual experiences, and declares the gracious dealings of God with his soul. While his lips, seasoned with grace, rehearsed the wondrous tale, his brethren, reminded of former seasons, find their dying hopes revive, the clouds of darkness flee away, and they cleave, in love, to God and one another. "Behold, how good and how pleasant it is for brethren to dwell together in unity!" (Ps. 133:1). "Not forsaking the assembling of ourselves together, as is the manner of some" (Heb. 10:25).

15

Separation

"Be separate" (2 Cor. 6:17), is a divine command, and as it becomes the members of churches to unite together, so it becomes them also to be separate from the world, as much as in them lies. They are "a garden enclosed" (Song 4:12), taken out of the wilderness of this world, and professed not to be of the world, but to be a distinct people, separated by the grace of God.

Let them then, like their divine master, be "separate from sinners" (Heb. 7:26). Entirely, they cannot, but let them not make carnal man their bosom friends, nor unnecessarily keep company with the wicked. Less to their sorrow they find that "their message will spread like cancer" (2 Tim. 2:17) and impair the vitals of religion.

It was said of Ephraim, "[He] has mixed himself among the peoples; Ephraim is a cake unturned. Aliens have devoured his strength, but he does not know it; yes, gray hairs are here and there on him, yet he does not know it" (Hos. 7:8–9). Ephraim had lost his strength, by keeping company with those that knew not God. The tokens of declension came imperceptibly upon him, "like a silly dove, without sense" (Hos. 7:11), that is, he was in some measure harmless, but had lost all his zeal, and had no heart for God.

My friends, "Do not be deceived: 'Evil company corrupts good habits'" (1 Cor. 15:33). "Therefore 'come out from among them, and be separate, says the Lord. Do not touch what is unclean'" (2 Cor. 6:17). But you say, "If I do this, I must forsake my relations, my friends, my father; I must give up all my worldly prospects." Well, be it so, the Lord says, "I will receive you. I will be a Father to you, and you shall be My sons and daughters" (2 Cor. 6:17–18). What a promise!

You shall be infinitely gainers by your loss! Trust in the Lord. Take him at His word. His promise never fails.

16

Holiness

In this, endeavor to be patterns to all around you that others behold "your good works and glorify your Father in heaven" (Matt. 5:16). Your Lord has said, "You shall be holy; for I am holy" (Lev. 11:44), and more will be expected from you than from many others, because you profess more.

As you are come out from the men of the world, see that your conduct be not like theirs. As you profess to be the disciples of Christ, imitate your great Master. Take heed to your steps. Be careful to fill up every character you bear, and every relation and connection in which you stand, with honor, and with a good conscience.

If you have parents, honor them. If you have masters, obey them. Have any of you unbelieving companions? Endeavor to win them by your good conversation. Are you masters? Threaten not your servants, but instruct them. Have you children? Endeavor to "bring them up in the training and admonition of the Lord" (Eph. 6:4).

Be careful to set a good example in your families. Let your houses be houses of prayer, lest the curse of God fall upon you. Give your servants no room to think they have a prayerless master. Nor your children to lament the want of a praying parent. Lest another day they should arise and curse you, but let every part of your conduct be such as shall teach them some good lesson of instruction.

Remember, you profess to be born from above, to be the sons and daughters of the Lord Almighty! Degrade not, then, your heavenly birth. Do not stab the cause which you profess. "Watch and pray, lest you enter into temptation" (Mark 14:38) and so fall from your profession. Brothers, "you are the temple of the living God. As God has said: 'I will dwell in them and walk among them'" (2 Cor. 6:16). Remember then, that "holiness adorns Your house, O Lord, forever" (Ps. 93:5).

17

Diligence

Diligence is becoming in every lawful calling, but most of all, in our high and heavenly calling because that is of the greatest consequence. Hence the Apostle says, "not lagging in diligence, fervent in spirit, serving the Lord" (Rom. 12:11).

An idle Christian is a strange sound; an indolent servant is almost a contradiction in terms. If we would therefore prove that we really are servants, we must lay aside our indolence, and "be even more diligent to make [our calling] and election sure" (2 Peter 1:10). And let us remember that Christ has said, "Not everyone who says to Me, "Lord, Lord," shall enter the kingdom of heaven, but he who does the will of my Father in heaven" (Matt. 7:21).

The affairs of your souls, brothers, are of the greatest importance, therefore they demand your utmost application. "What will a man give in exchange for his soul?" (Matt. 16:26). If your souls are lost, all is lost. Surely, he that neglects the concerns of his soul is a stranger to the worth of it.

I would wish you also to remember, brothers, that to every particular duty which has been inculcated, you are to add diligence, and to exercise it in them all so you may escape the odious name of Slothful Servants. The awful portion of such as hide their talent in a napkin.

Be diligent, then, in every duty. For your encouragement, remember, God has said, "Those who wait on the Lord shall renew their strength; they shall mount up with wings like eagles, they shall run and not be weary, they shall walk and not faint" (Is. 40:31). Let your grand aim be, so to act, as you may at the last day obtain the approbation of the great Judge of all the earth. So run that you may obtain, "as many as walk according to this rule, peace and mercy be upon them, and upon the Israel of God" (Gal. 6:16).

18

Address to a Brother Being Appointed to the Office of Deacon

My dear Brother! Permit me to add, it will be expected that you, in a particular manner, should be diligent in all these duties as you are appointed to an office in the church of God. The eyes of your fellow members will be upon you, and it is hoped you will set them an example of holiness and diligence.

Do not confine your views of the office to which you are appointed to secular and financial matters. For if these be the only things which you are to attend to, why are such particular qualifications required in a deacon? Almost any honest man might have filled up the office, and they needed not to have chosen men "full of the Holy Spirit and wisdom" (Acts 6:3). Visit the sick, and pray with them; and give evidence to all around you that yours is that "pure and undefiled religion" which teaches "to visit orphans and widows in their trouble, and to keep oneself unspotted from the world" (James 1:27).

In a word, endeavor to be a nursing father to this little people and help forward such as you may see waiting at the doors of God's house. May God grant that you may see prosperity, and that your own soul may prosper.

Conclusion

"So now, brethren, I commend you to God and to the word of His grace, which is able to build you up and give you an inheritance among all those who are sanctified" (Acts 20:32). May the blessing of God almighty, the Father, Son, and Holy Spirit, rest upon you. May you be increased into a multitude. When your lips shall lay silent in the grave, and this generation pass away, may your children, and your children's children, be a seed to serve the Lord, throughout all generations, "till He comes" (1 Cor. 11:26). To Him be glory, both now, and forever. Amen, and Amen.

Bibliography

"A List, for 1791, etc. Of the Principal Books and Pamphlets which have been lately printed by the Baptists" in John Rippon, *The Baptist Annual Register, for 1790, 1791, 1792, and Part of 1793* (London, 1793), 331.

"A List of Some of the Books and Pamphlets Lately Published by the Baptists, [1794]" in John Rippon, *The Baptist Annual Register, for 1794, 1795, 1796–1797* (London, 1797), 222.

"Account of Religious Publications: *Christian Duties Recommended, etc. By Zenas Trivett*," *The Baptist Magazine* 6 (1814): 169.

An Account of the Bristol Education Society: For the Year Ending June, 1805 (Bristol: Harris and Bryan, 1805), 8 and 21.

An Account of the Bristol Education Society: For the Year Ending June, 1806 (Bristol: Harris and Bryan, 1806), 8.

An Account of the Bristol Education Society: For the Year Ending June, 1807 (Bristol: Harris and Bryan, 1807), 8.

An Account of the Bristol Education Society: For the Year Ending June, 1815 (Bristol: Mary Bryan, 1815), 7.

"Church at Thorpe, in Essex" in John Rippon, *The Baptist Annual Register, for 1801 and 1802* (London, 1802), 1147.

"Domestic Religious Intelligence: English Baptist Associations," *The Baptist Magazine* 5 (1813): 387.

"English Associations: Norfolk and Suffolk Associations. 1797 and 1798" in John Rippon, *The Baptist Annual Register, for 1798, 1799, 1800, and Part of 1801* (London, 1801), 81.

"Extracts from the Circular Letter to The Baptist Churches in Essex" in John Rippon, *The Baptist Annual Register, for 1801 and 1802* (London, 1802), 580–581.

"Memoir of the Late Rev. Joseph Kinghorn," *The Evangelical Magazine and Missionary Chronicle*, n.s. 10 (1832): 510.

"Memoir of the Rev. Thomas Steevens," *The Baptist Magazine* 9 (1817): 87.

"Norfolk and Suffolk Association, 1794" in John Rippon, *The Baptist Annual Register, for 1794, 1795, 1796–1797* (London, 1797), 188.

"Obituary. Mr. Edward Rogers" in John Rippon, *The Baptist Annual Register, for 1801 and 1802* (London, 1802), 830.

"Obituary: Rev. Zenas Trivett," *The Baptist Magazine* 23 (1831): 537–538.

"Ordinations in 1790, 1791, 1792: Rev. John Hutchings" in John Rippon, *The Baptist Annual Register for 1790, 1791, 1792, and Part of 1793* (London, 1793), 519.

"Religious Intelligence: General Association of Baptist Churches," *The Baptist Magazine* 4 (1812): 358.

"Will of Zenas Trivett, Dissenting Minister of North Walsham, Norfolk" (**PROB** 11/1797/436), The National Archives.

Brackett, W. "Success of Village Preaching in Essex" in John Rippon, *The Baptist Annual Register, for 1798, 1799, 1800, and Part of 1801* (London, 1801), 186.

Compton, J. E. "Colchester and the Missionary Movement," *The Baptist Quarterly*, 11 (1941–1945): 55.

Fuller, Andrew. "Extracts from the Late Rev. A. Fuller's Correspondence with the Late Rev. Mr. Steevens, of Colchester," *The Baptist Magazine* 8 (1816): 454–455.

Hewett, Maurice F. "Early Days at Worstead," *The Baptist Quarterly* 11 (1941–1945): 168–170.

[Hutchings, John ?]. "The Baptist Association in Essex, for Itinerant and Village Preaching" in John Rippon, *The Baptist Annual Register, for 1794, 1795, 1796–1797* (London, 1797), 484.

Ivimey, Joseph. *A History of the English Baptists* (London: Isaac Taylor Hinton and Holdsworth & Ball, 1830), IV, 125 and 524.

Price, Seymour J. "The Early Years of the Baptist Union," *The Baptist Quarterly* 4 (1928–1929): 58.

Trivett, Zenas. *Plain Christian Duties Recommended* (Sudbury: W. Brackett, 1791).

———. *Plain Christian Duties Recommended*, 2nd ed. (London: W. Button, 1791).

———. *A Scheme of Chronology representing at one View, the Times of the Prophets, and how long they Prophesied* (1794).

GRACE BIBLE
THEOLOGICAL
SEMINARY

Interested in becoming a student
or supporting our ministry?
Please visit gbtseminary.org